D1288884

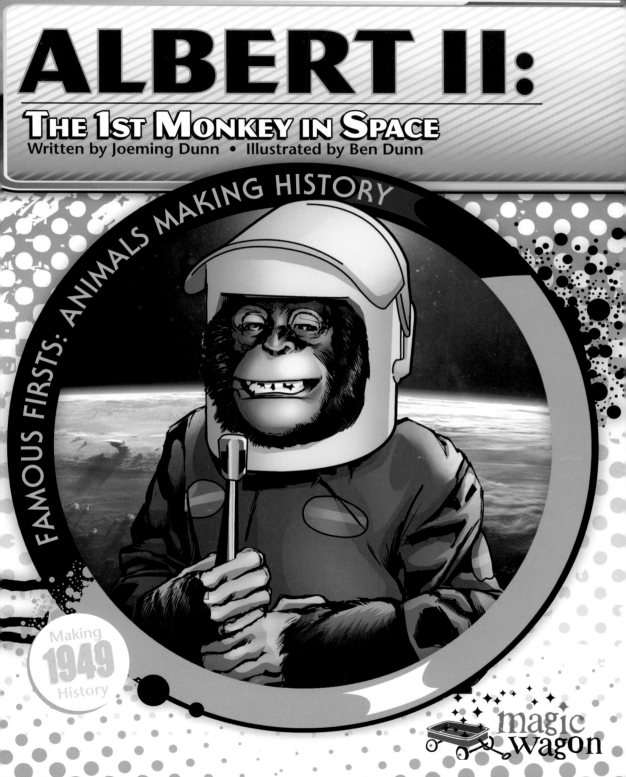

ALBERT II:

THE 1ST MONKEY IN SPACE

Written by Joeming Dunn • Illustrated by Ben Dunn

FAMOUS FIRSTS: ANIMALS MAKING HISTORY

Making 1949 History

magic wagon

visit us at www.abdopublishing.com

Published by Magic Wagon, a division of the ABDO Publishing Group, 8000 West 78th Street, Edina, Minnesota 55439. Copyright © 2012 by Abdo Consulting Group, Inc. International copyrights reserved in all countries. All rights reserved. No part of this book may be reproduced in any form without written permission from the publisher.

Graphic Planet™ is a trademark and logo of Magic Wagon.

Printed in the United States of America, North Mankato, Minnesota.
052011
092011
This book contains at least 10% recycled materials.

Written by Joeming Dunn
Illustrated by Ben Dunn
Colored by Robby Bevard
Lettered by Doug Dlin
Edited by Stephanie Hedlund and Rochelle Baltzer
Interior layout and design by Antarctic Press
Cover art by Brian Denham
Cover design by Neil Klinepier

Library of Congress Cataloging-in-Publication Data

Dunn, Joeming W.
  Albert II : the 1st monkey in space / written by Joeming Dunn ; Illustrated by Ben Dunn.
      p. cm. -- (Famous firsts. Animals making history)
  Includes index.
  ISBN 978-1-61641-637-9
  1. Albert II (Monkey)--Juvenile literature. 2. Animal space flight--Juvenile literature.
3. Monkeys as laboratory animals--Juvenile literature. 4. Astronautics--United States--History--
20th century. I. Dunn, Ben, ill. II. Title.
  TL793.D86 2012
  629.450092'9--dc22
                          2011010679

TABLE OF CONTENTS

Dreams of Space 5

Beginnings of Rocketry 9

Weapon of War. 15

Early Days of Space Exploration 20

Animals in Space. 24

Albert II Facts 30

Web Sites 30

Glossary 31

Index 32

Humans have always dreamed of reaching the stars. Early civilizations worshipped the objects in the sky. In many cultures, the sun and the moon were seen as gods.

In the 1000s, the Chinese developed flimsy rockets. They were made of paper and gunpowder and were used as weapons.

Later, in the 1600s and 1700s, Europeans began to change the rocket. They started building them with iron and were able to add a payload.

As we began to understand the universe a little bit more, a lot of people started to dream of going into space.

Authors, including Jules Verne, wrote adventures about going to the moon.

In 1865, Verne wrote the book *From the Earth to the Moon*. In it, a spaceship was launched to the moon using a giant cannon.

H.G. Wells wrote about space travelers and Martian invaders in his book *War of the Worlds*.

While many dreamed of space travel, Russian scientist Konstantin Tsiolkovsky worked to make it happen. He was the first to create a practical design for a rocket.

Tsiolkovsky realized it would take a certain speed to escape Earth's gravity.

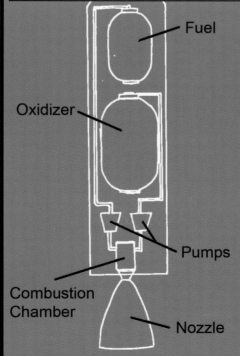

He went on to suggest an engine that could do this. It would have solid fuel, which would cause a combustion reaction that would propel the rocket upward.

Fuel

Oxidizer

Pumps

Combustion Chamber

Nozzle

WE NEED TO CREATE A NEW FUEL. IT WILL NEED TO HAVE A CHEMICAL ADDED TO HELP IT BURN.

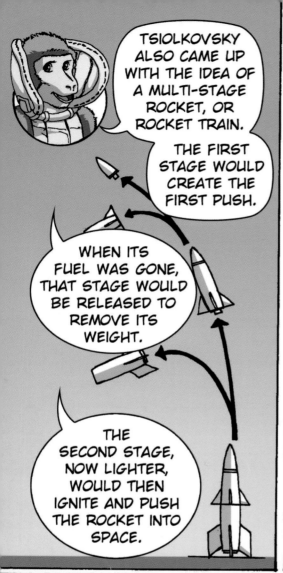

TSIOLKOVSKY ALSO CAME UP WITH THE IDEA OF A MULTI-STAGE ROCKET, OR ROCKET TRAIN.

THE FIRST STAGE WOULD CREATE THE FIRST PUSH.

WHEN ITS FUEL WAS GONE, THAT STAGE WOULD BE RELEASED TO REMOVE ITS WEIGHT.

THE SECOND STAGE, NOW LIGHTER, WOULD THEN IGNITE AND PUSH THE ROCKET INTO SPACE.

An American scientist named Robert Goddard expanded upon Tsiolkovsky's work.

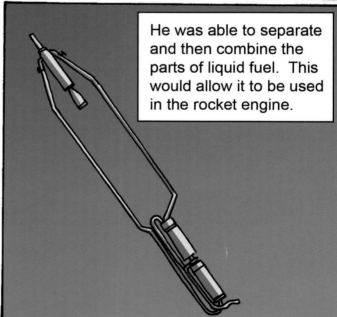

He was able to separate and then combine the parts of liquid fuel. This would allow it to be used in the rocket engine.

Goddard wrote a book called *A Method of Reaching Extreme Altitudes*. But a *New York Times* newspaper article in 1920 made fun of him.

The paper retracted its statement when man landed on the moon in 1969.

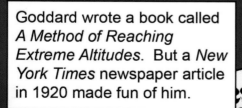

BEGINNINGS OF ROCKETRY

Goddard continued to work on his ideas. On March 16, 1926, his liquid-fuel rocket, named *Neil*, took flight. It reached a height of 41 feet (12 m) in two and half seconds.

Soon, many people were experimenting with rockets.

Many "rocket societies" were formed so engineers and physicists could gather to develop new types of rockets.

Much of the rocketry basics began with Goddard and Tsiolkovsky. But it was the visions of German Hermann Oberth that spurred the idea of space travel.

Oberth's books, *The Rocket of Interplanetary Space* and *Ways to Spaceflight*, were generally accepted.

It helped that Oberth acted as an adviser for a movie called *Frau im Mond* (*The Woman in the Moon*).

His work inspired other scientists to work together. They formed even more groups or societies to work on their ideas.

One German rocket society was the VfR or *Verein fur Raumschiffahrt*, which means Society for Space Travel.

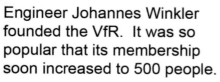

Engineer Johannes Winkler founded the VfR. It was so popular that its membership soon increased to 500 people.

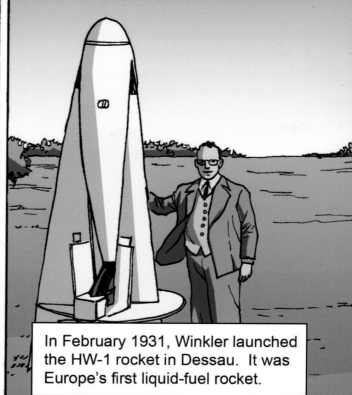

In February 1931, Winkler launched the HW-1 rocket in Dessau. It was Europe's first liquid-fuel rocket.

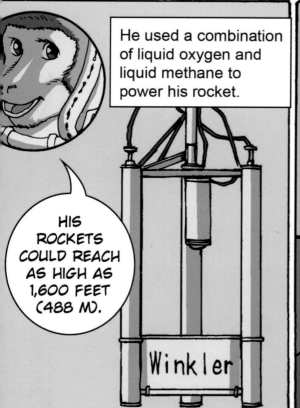

He used a combination of liquid oxygen and liquid methane to power his rocket.

HIS ROCKETS COULD REACH AS HIGH AS 1,600 FEET (488 M).

Winkler

Other VfR members, such as Rudolf Nebel and Klaus Riedel, continued to improve on the design.

Soon their rockets were going as high as 3,500 feet (1,067 m).

The VfR's work caught the interest of a German army captain named Walter Dornberger.

I THINK THERE ARE POSSIBLE MILITARY USES IN YOUR RESEARCH.

I NEED A GROUP TO WORK IN SECRET AND CONCENTRATE ON ROCKET WEAPONRY.

In return for their work with Dornberger, the VfR would get funding.

Many in the society did not want to accept these conditions. It nearly tore the society apart.

It soon didn't matter. Within the year, the Nazi party took control of the German government and outlawed civilian rocket experiments and testing. Soon after, many in the VfR were recruited to work for the army.

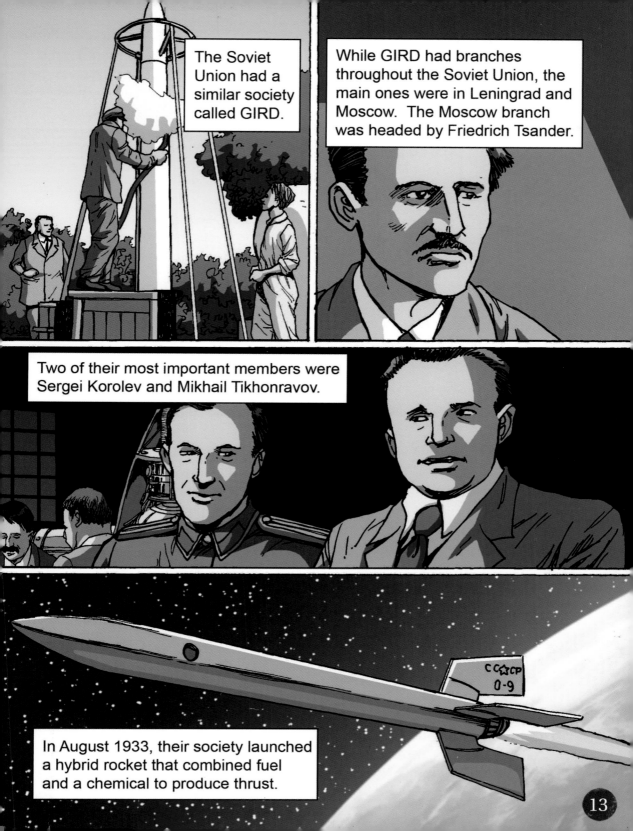

The Soviet Union had a similar society called GIRD.

While GIRD had branches throughout the Soviet Union, the main ones were in Leningrad and Moscow. The Moscow branch was headed by Friedrich Tsander.

Two of their most important members were Sergei Korolev and Mikhail Tikhonravov.

In August 1933, their society launched a hybrid rocket that combined fuel and a chemical to produce thrust.

Soon, GIRD launched a rocket powered by alcohol and liquid. It reached a height of 250 feet (76 m).

GIRD was constantly monitored by the Soviet state. Their success drew the attention of Red Army Field Marshal Mikhail Tukhachevsky.

Tukhachevsky joined GIRD with the Gas Dynamic Laboratory (GDL) to form the Jet Propulsion Research Institute (RNII).

Unfortunately, the new organization had many internal problems. After many from GIRD were executed as traitors to the state, the Soviet Union program fell apart.

Walter Dornberger was a World War I veteran who had studied physics for many years. He also was in charge of a weapons testing facility at West Kummersdorf, Germany.

He championed a rocket that could be used to launch a payload to a potential target.

He began to work on some designs. After some initial failures, he soon developed a pair of A2 rockets, which he called Max and Moritz. They used ethyl alcohol and liquid oxygen as fuel.

Many in the original VfR society rejected military money. But, one of the up-and-coming scientists, Wernher von Braun, saw its value to future research.

15

Von Braun's designs included a new feature. He included a system of spinning gyroscopes that helped steady the entire rocket and maintain a stable flight.

A GYROSCOPE IS A SPINNING DISK OR WHEEL MOUNTED ON A BASE.

ITS AXIS CAN FREELY TURN IN ONE OR MORE DIRECTIONS AND STAY POINTED IN THE SAME DIRECTION, NO MATTER THE MOVEMENT OF THE BASE.

As Nazi Germany was preparing for war, there was added pressure to develop a rocket for fighting.

It would have to contain an explosive warhead and carry it a distance to strike the enemy.

TNT

The Germans would use these rockets as missiles to strike Great Britain during the war.

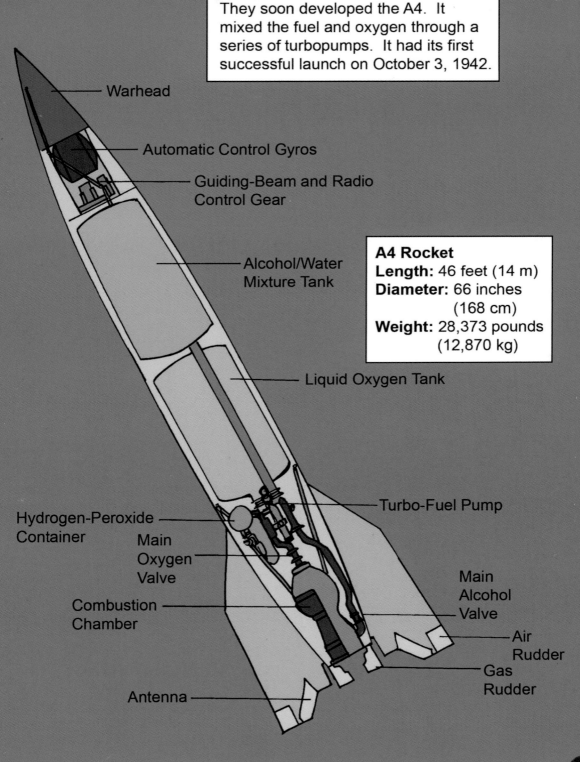

They soon developed the A4. It mixed the fuel and oxygen through a series of turbopumps. It had its first successful launch on October 3, 1942.

Warhead

Automatic Control Gyros

Guiding-Beam and Radio Control Gear

Alcohol/Water Mixture Tank

A4 Rocket
Length: 46 feet (14 m)
Diameter: 66 inches (168 cm)
Weight: 28,373 pounds (12,870 kg)

Liquid Oxygen Tank

Turbo-Fuel Pump

Hydrogen-Peroxide Container

Main Oxygen Valve

Combustion Chamber

Main Alcohol Valve

Air Rudder

Gas Rudder

Antenna

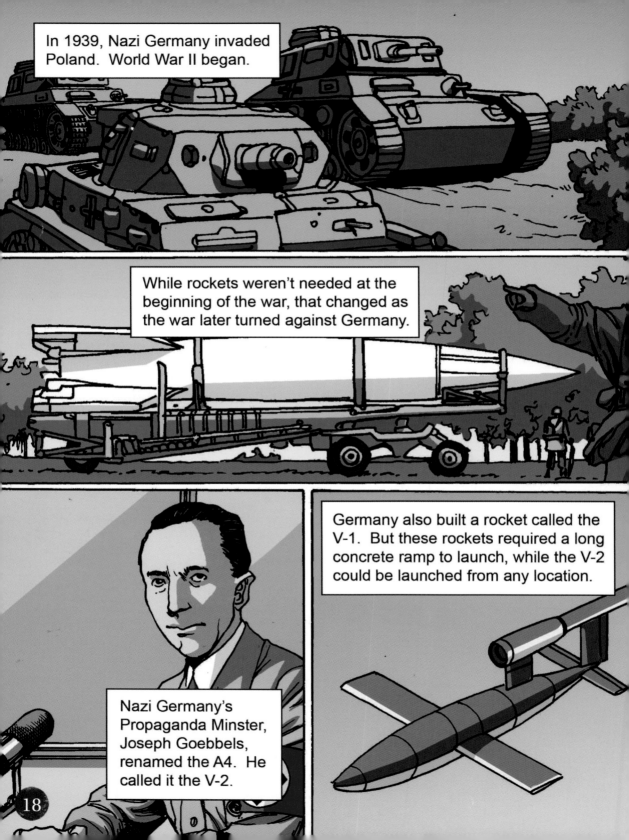

In 1939, Nazi Germany invaded Poland. World War II began.

While rockets weren't needed at the beginning of the war, that changed as the war later turned against Germany.

Germany also built a rocket called the V-1. But these rockets required a long concrete ramp to launch, while the V-2 could be launched from any location.

Nazi Germany's Propaganda Minster, Joseph Goebbels, renamed the A4. He called it the V-2.

The first V-1s were fired on London in June 1944. The British nicknamed them "buzz bombs" for the sound they made as they traveled in the sky.

The V-2 was fired soon after, in September.

Once fired, the V-2 would shoot up and then would fall, striking a populated area. The V-2s were not very accurate, so they were aimed at large cities. Because the rockets fell silently, most people didn't even know they were fired until they struck. This made the V-2 a very frightening weapon.

Over 3,000 attacks were made with these weapons.

Fortunately, Allied bombing and the Allied invasion of Europe drove the Nazi army back. The target cities were soon out of range of these weapons. The Nazi rule ended soon afterward.

Both the United States and the Soviet Union saw the advances the Germans had made in rocket development.

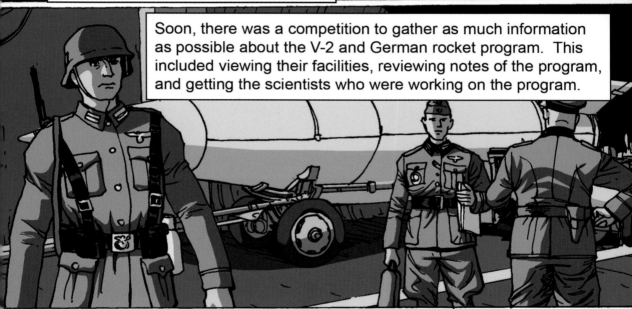

Soon, there was a competition to gather as much information as possible about the V-2 and German rocket program. This included viewing their facilities, reviewing notes of the program, and getting the scientists who were working on the program.

Wernher von Braun was captured and, after careful negotiations, was sent to the United States. He was stationed with other scientists at Fort Bliss, Texas, forming the beginning of the US Space Program.

But the Soviet Union had also gained key scientists, such as Helmut Grottrup. They were also first to capture the cities where the V-2s were being produced.

Soon, many of the scientists with von Braun gathered together and began development of American rockets under Operation Overcast.

People were very suspicious because of von Braun's connection with the Nazis. This made work extremely slow.

Von Braun soon proved himself a promoter for rocket science and space exploration.

In the early days of the Space Race, military superiority and missiles were considered more important than research for space exploration.

The early months at Fort Bliss were slow. The budget for the project was small, so there wasn't a lot to spend for equipment and research.

J. Edgar Hoover, the head of the FBI, feared the influence of the Nazis. He considered the scientists to be security risks.

Despite the occasional roadblock, scientists still had interest in going into space.

Early on, almost all scientists knew the dangers of spaceflight.

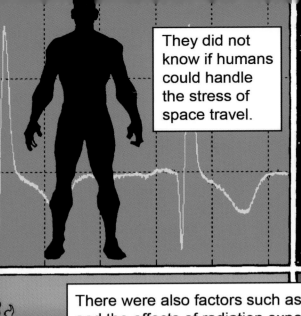

They did not know if humans could handle the stress of space travel.

They also weren't sure how humans would react to weightlessness.

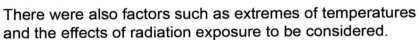

There were also factors such as extremes of temperatures and the effects of radiation exposure to be considered.

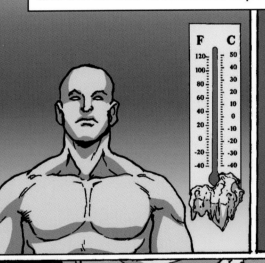

RADIATION

THIS IS WHERE I COME IN!

The first living things to be sent up in a rocket were fruit flies and plants, including moss and corn seed. These missions were used to study the effects of radiation in space on living things.

Since there were many concerns about humans in space, both the United States and Soviet Union used animals for testing.

Several types of monkeys were chosen for the space program as well. They included rhesus, Philippine, squirrel, and pigtail macaque monkeys.

The first mammal to be sent skyward was Albert I. He was a rhesus monkey.

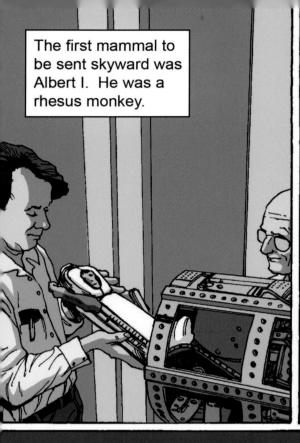

On June 11, 1948, Albert I was sent up on a V-2 rocket. He rode up to a height of 39 miles (63 km). Unfortunately, Albert I passed away during his flight. Most believe it was from suffocation.

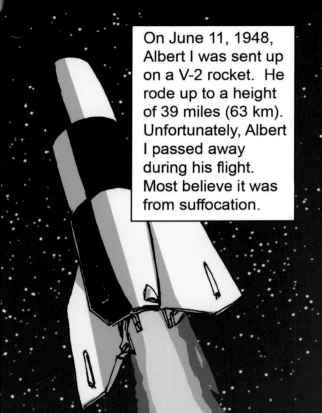

This was where I joined the Space Age! I was the second monkey chosen to head for the stars. My mission was quite important, because I would go higher than Albert I.

I was a rhesus monkey, too. There isn't much other information known about me.

My mission soon came, and I was prepped for launch. I was given some medicine to help me relax for my trip.

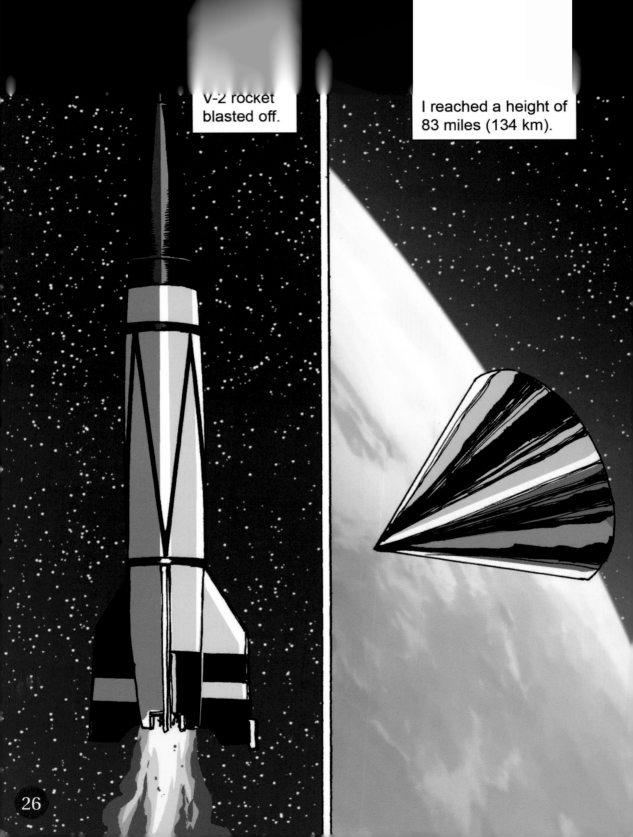

V-2 rocket blasted off.

I reached a height of 83 miles (134 km).

At the time, I reached above the Kármán line. That is an altitude about 62 miles (100 km) above Earth's sea level.

So I became the first mammal in space!

My mission did not last long before I returned to Earth.

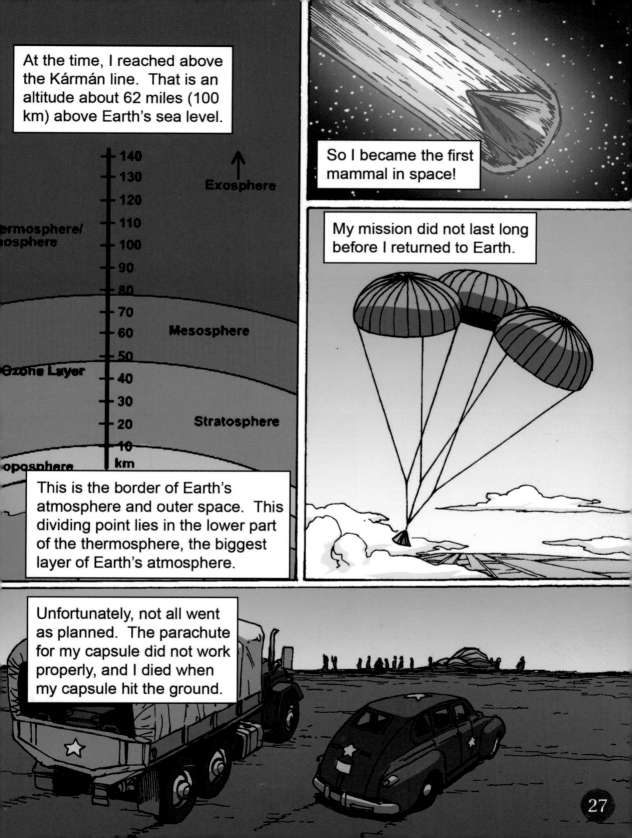

140
130
120
Exosphere
110
ermosphere/
hosphere
100
90
80
70
60
Mesosphere
50
Ozone Layer
40
30
20
Stratosphere
10
km
oposphere

This is the border of Earth's atmosphere and outer space. This dividing point lies in the lower part of the thermosphere, the biggest layer of Earth's atmosphere.

Unfortunately, not all went as planned. The parachute for my capsule did not work properly, and I died when my capsule hit the ground.

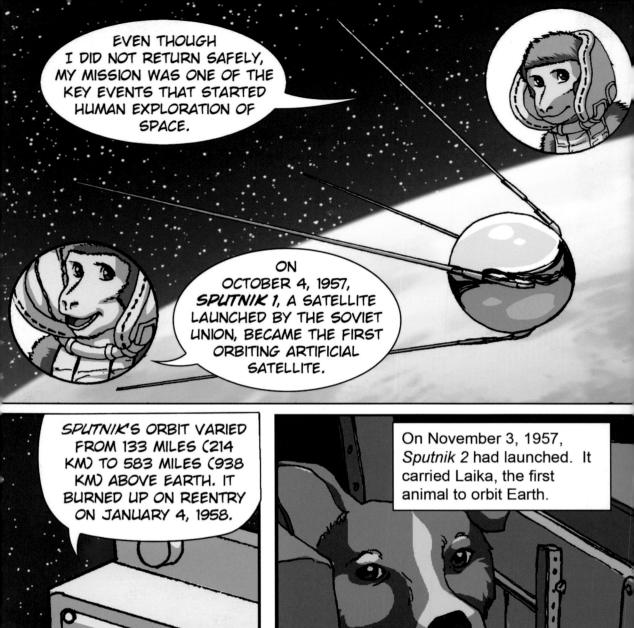

EVEN THOUGH I DID NOT RETURN SAFELY, MY MISSION WAS ONE OF THE KEY EVENTS THAT STARTED HUMAN EXPLORATION OF SPACE.

ON OCTOBER 4, 1957, *SPUTNIK 1*, A SATELLITE LAUNCHED BY THE SOVIET UNION, BECAME THE FIRST ORBITING ARTIFICIAL SATELLITE.

SPUTNIK'S ORBIT VARIED FROM 133 MILES (214 KM) TO 583 MILES (938 KM) ABOVE EARTH. IT BURNED UP ON REENTRY ON JANUARY 4, 1958.

On November 3, 1957, *Sputnik* 2 had launched. It carried Laika, the first animal to orbit Earth.

THE SPACE RACE HAD BEGUN!

28

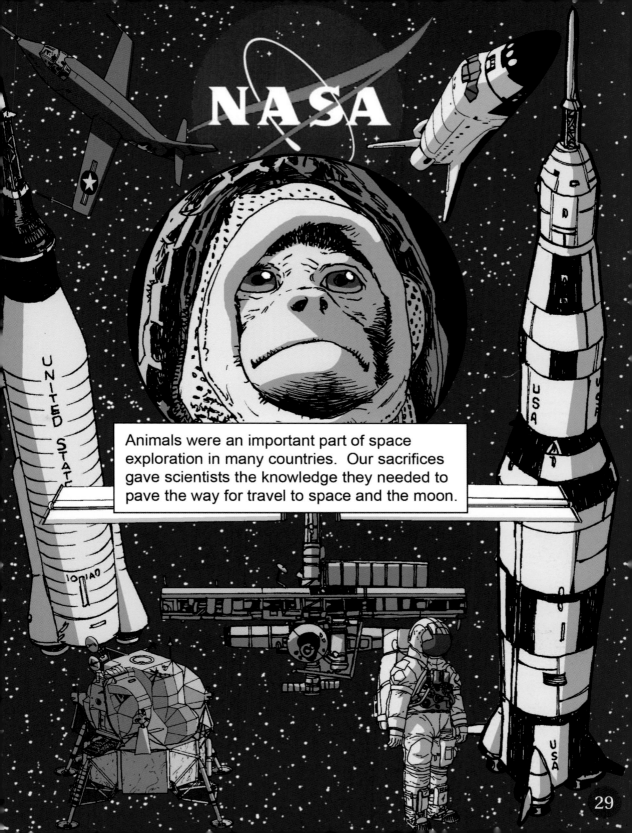

Animals were an important part of space exploration in many countries. Our sacrifices gave scientists the knowledge they needed to pave the way for travel to space and the moon.

ALBERT II FACTS

Name: Albert the Second

Age at the time of the journey: Unknown

Weight: Unknown

Breed: Rhesus monkey of the Air Force Aero Medical Laboratory

Launch date: June 14, 1949

Launch site: White Sands Proving Grounds, New Mexico

Launch height: 83 miles (134 km)

Result: Sensors monitored Albert II's heartbeat, blood pressure, and other bodily functions to better understand the physical changes that might happen in space. His flight proved space travel was possible.

Making 1949 History

WEB SITES

To learn more about Albert II, visit ABDO Group online at **www.abdopublishing.com**. Web sites about Albert II are featured on our Book Links page. These links are routinely monitored and updated to provide the most current information available.

GLOSSARY

allies – people or countries that agree to help each other in times of need. During World War II Great Britain, France, the United States, and the Soviet Union were called the Allies.

atmosphere – the layer of air surrounding Earth.

capsule – a small compartment in a vehicle that is pressurized for spaceflight.

combustion reaction – when a compound is mixed with oxygen it produces carbon dioxide and water, which produces heat.

ethyl alcohol – an organic compound used as an important industrial chemical.

gravity – the force that pulls a smaller object toward a larger object.

hybrid – combining two or more functions or ways of operation.

ignite – to set on fire.

methane – a colorless, odorless natural gas.

missile – a weapon that is thrown or projected to hit a target.

Nazi – a member of the German political party that controlled Germany under Adolf Hitler.

payload – the people and instruments carried by a vehicle that is needed for its flight.

physicist – a person who studies matter and energy and how they affect each other.

retract – to withdraw.

sacrifice – something given up or lost for the sake of something else.

satellite – a manufactured object that orbits Earth. It relays weather and scientific information back to Earth. It also sends television programs across Earth.

superiority – to be better, higher, or greater than something or someone.

suspicious – causing a feeling that something is wrong.

thermosphere – the uppermost layer of Earth's atmosphere.

thrust – a force from a jet or a rocket engine that moves the vehicle forward.

INDEX

A
Allies 19
animal testing 24, 25, 26, 27, 28, 29

B
Braun, Wernher von 15, 16, 20, 21

C
China 5

D
death 27
Dornberger, Walter 12, 15

E
England 19

F
fuel 7, 8, 9, 11, 13, 14, 15, 17

G
Germany 9, 10, 11, 12, 15, 16, 18, 20
GIRD 13, 14
Goddard, Robert 8, 9
Goebbels, Joseph 18
gravity 7
Grottrup, Helmut 20
gyroscopes 16

H
Hoover, J. Edgar 22

J
Jet Propulsion Research Institute 14

K
Kármán line 27
Korolev, Sergei 13

M
moon 5, 6, 8, 28

N
Nazis 12, 16, 18, 19, 21, 22
Nebel, Rudolf 11

O
Oberth, Hermann 9, 10
Operation Overcast 21

P
Poland 18

R
radiation 23, 24
Riedel, Klaus 11
rocket societies 9, 10, 11, 12, 13

rockets 5, 7, 8, 9, 10, 11, 12, 13, 14, 15, 16, 17, 18, 19, 20, 21, 25, 26
Russia 7

S
Soviet Union 13, 14, 20, 24, 28
Sputnik 28
sun 5

T
Tikhonravov, Mikhail 13
Tsander, Friedrich 13
Tsiolkovsky, Konstantin 7, 8, 9
Tukhachevsky, Mikhail 14

U
United States 20, 21, 24

V
Verne, Jules 6
VfR 10, 11, 12, 15

W
Wells, H.G. 6
Winkler, Johannes 11
World War II 18